NEW! **LOOK FOR THE CAMERA** in our instru
technique videos made just for you! **www.Le**

MW00659344

The Cuffed Shawl and More!

So easy to crochet and so appealing on women of all sizes and shapes, these unique designs are today's must-have fashions! Optional features lend lots of versatility to the four basic wraps.

LEISURE ARTS, INC. • Maumelle, Arkansas

cuffed shawl

EASY

A wonderfully comfortable cross between a shawl and a sweater, this design is crocheted in two pieces and sewn together up the back. Added cuffs and short seams form loose sleeves that help keep the shawl in place. You can even make it a hoodie. The size can be easily adjusted, but be sure to buy yarn accordingly.

Finished Size: Approximately 29" long (73.5 cm) x 53" (134.5 cm) cuff to cuff

SHOPPING LIST

Yarn (Bulky Weight) BULKY 5

Plain Neckline

[3 ounces, 144 yards (85 grams, 132 meters) per skein]:

- ☐ 8 skeins

With Hood

[6 ounces, 185 yards (170 grams, 169 meters) per skein]:

- ☐ 6 skeins

Crochet Hook

- ☐ Size K (6.5 mm) **or** size needed for gauge

Additional Supplies

- ☐ Yarn needle
- ☐ 1½" - 2" (38 mm - 51 mm) Button
- ☐ Pins

GAUGE INFORMATION

10 dc and 6 rows = 4" (10 cm)

Gauge Swatch: 4" (10 cm) square

Ch 12.

Row 1: Dc in third ch from hook and in each ch across: 10 dc.

Beginning ch 2 does **not** count as a dc.

Rows 2-6: Ch 2, turn; dc in each dc across.

Finish off.

STITCH GUIDE

DOUBLE CROCHET 2 TOGETHER

(abbreviated dc2tog)

(uses 2 dc)

★ YO, insert hook in **next** dc, YO and pull up a loop, YO and draw through 2 loops on hook; repeat from ★ once **more**, YO and draw through all 3 loops on hook (**counts as one dc**).

The Body is worked in two separate pieces. Each piece begins at the wrist and is worked to the center back of the garment, increasing stitches on each edge. The two pieces will be sewn together across a portion of the last row, forming the center back seam.

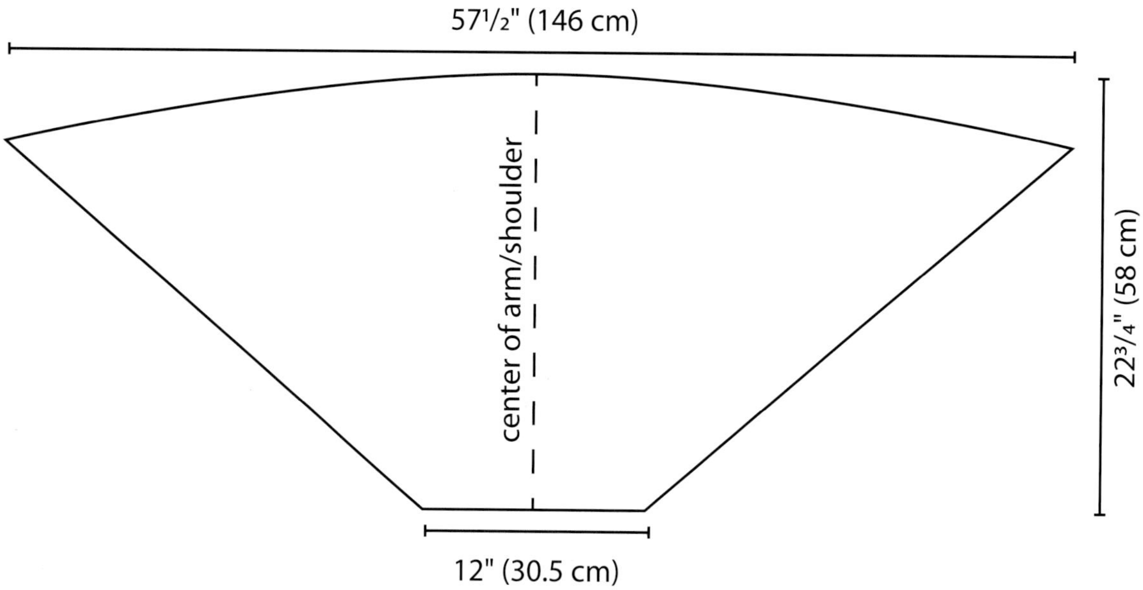

INSTRUCTIONS

BODY (Make 2)

Ch 32.

Row 1 (Right side)**:** Dc in third ch from hook and in each ch across: 30 dc.

Note: Loop a short piece of yarn around any dc on Row 1 to mark **right** side.

Beginning ch 2 does **not** count as a dc.

Rows 2-10 (Increase rows)**:** Ch 2, turn; 2 dc in first dc, dc in each remaining dc across to last dc, 2 dc in last dc: 48 dc.

Row 11 (Increase row)**:** Ch 2, turn; 2 dc in first dc, dc in next 9 dc, 2 dc in next dc, (dc in next 8 dc, 2 dc in next dc) 3 times, dc in next 9 dc, 2 dc in last dc: 54 dc.

Row 12 (Increase row)**:** Ch 2, turn; 2 dc in first dc, dc in each remaining dc across to last dc, 2 dc in last dc: 56 dc.

Row 13 (Increase row)**:** Ch 2, turn; 2 dc in first dc, dc in next 12 dc, 2 dc in next dc, (dc in next 9 dc, 2 dc in next dc) 3 times, dc in next 11 dc, 2 dc in last dc: 62 dc.

Row 14 (Increase row)**:** Ch 2, turn; 2 dc in first dc, dc in each remaining dc across to last dc, 2 dc in last dc: 64 dc.

Row 15 (Increase row)**:** Work in same manner as Row 13, increasing in first and last dc with 4 more increases evenly spaced between: 70 dc.

The fabulous drape of the Cuffed Shawl flatters women of all shapes and sizes!

Rows 16-34: Repeat Rows 14 and 15, 9 times; then repeat Row 14 once **more**: 144 dc.

At this point the size can be adjusted. Drape the long edge over one shoulder, allowing the beginning row to rest at your wrist. Keep in mind that you will be adding a 3" (7.5 cm) cuff. If the length is satisfactory, finish off. If you would like it longer and wider, continue to add rows in same manner, then finish off.

PLACEMENT DIAGRAM

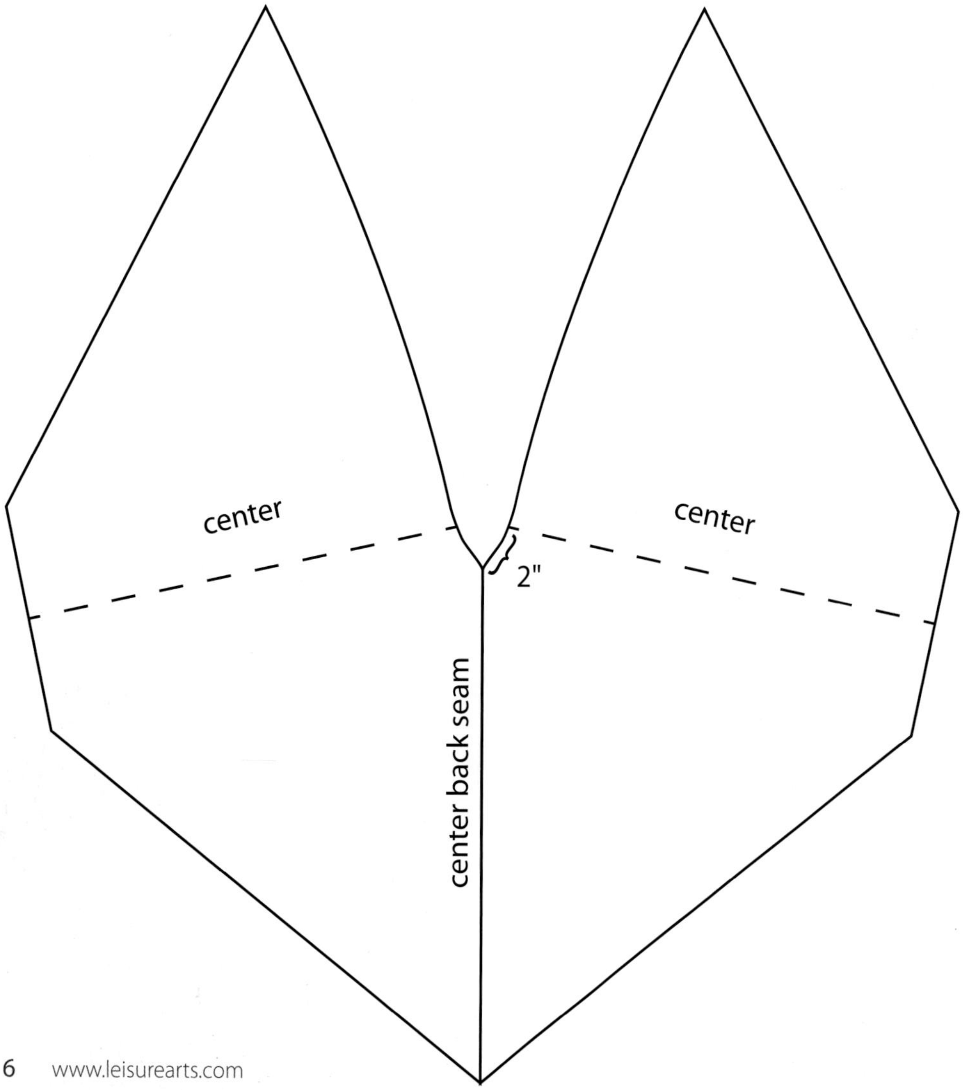

ASSEMBLY

Place Body pieces with **wrong** sides together. Using the placement diagram as a guide, pin pieces together across the last row to about 2" (5 cm) before the center.

Note: If you are making the shawl with a textured yarn, it may be easier to sew the seam using a smooth yarn.

Working through **both** loops of **both** pieces, whipstitch Body pieces together ***(Fig. 6a, page 31)***, keeping the sewing yarn fairly loose.

CUFF

Row 1: With **right** side facing and working in free loops of beginning ch on one side of Body ***(Fig. 2, page 30)***, join yarn with slip st in first ch; ch 9, sc in second ch from hook and in each ch across; slip st in next 2 chs on Body: 8 sc.

Row 2: Ch 1, turn; skip first 2 slip sts, sc in Back Loop Only of each sc across ***(Fig. 1, page 30)***.

Row 3: Ch 1, turn; sc in Back Loop Only of each sc across; slip st in next 2 chs on Body.

Rows 4-28: Repeat Rows 2 and 3, 12 times; then repeat Row 2 once **more**.

Row 29: Ch 1, turn; sc in Back Loop Only of each sc across; slip st in last ch on Body, finish off.

With **wrong** sides together and beginning at edge of Cuff, whipstitch first and last rows of Cuff together; then whipstitch across end of rows on Body for 3" (7.5 cm) if desired ***(Fig. 6b, page 31)***.

HOOD

Row 1: With **right** side facing, count 22 dc from seam and join yarn with dc in same st *(Fig. 4, page 31)*; dc in next 21 dc (on same Body piece) and in next 22 dc on second Body piece: 44 dc.

Rows 2-20: Ch 2, turn; dc in each dc across.

Row 21: Ch 2, turn; dc in first 20 dc, dc2tog twice, dc in each remaining dc across: 42 dc.

Row 22: Ch 2, turn; dc in first 19 dc, dc2tog twice, dc in each remaining dc across; finish off leaving a long end for sewing Hood seam: 40 dc.

Fold Hood in half with **wrong** side together and matching dc on last row; whipstitch top seam.

FRONT BAND

Row 1: With **right** side facing, join yarn with sc in bottom corner of front edge *(Figs. 3a & b, page 30)*, sc in each remaining dc across Body; sc evenly across end of rows on Hood if it was added; sc in each dc across Body.

Row 2: Ch 1, turn; sc in each sc across.

Place a marker for buttonhole placement in sc 3½" (9 cm) from Hood, **or** 12¼" (31 cm) from seam on a plain neckline.

Row 3: Ch 1, turn; sc in each sc across to marked sc, ch 3, skip next 3 sc **(buttonhole made)**, sc in each remaining sc across.

Row 4: Ch 1, turn; sc in each sc across working 3 sc in ch-3 sp.

Row 5: Ch 1, turn; sc in each sc across; finish off.

Sew button on opposite front matching buttonhole.

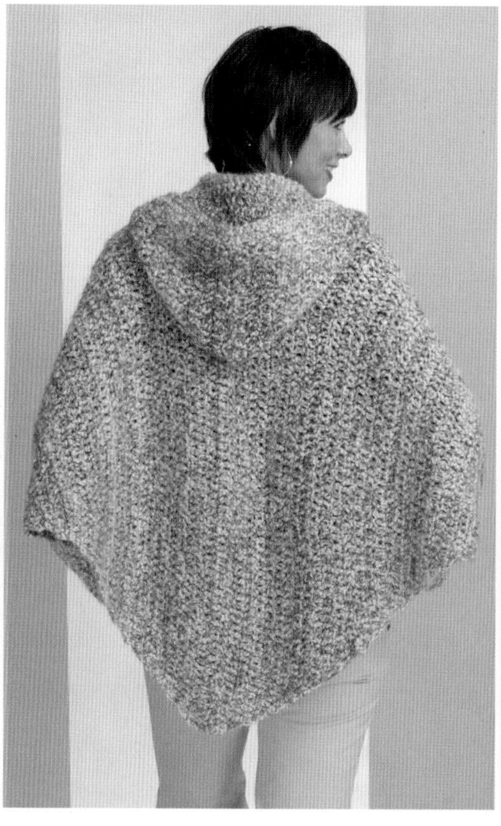

ruffled shawl

EASY

This simple triangular shawl has a unique jacket variation.
Loose, short sleeves are formed when you button up the side edges.

Finished Size: Approximately 62$^{1}/_{2}$" wide x 25$^{1}/_{2}$" deep at the center point (159 cm x 65 cm)

SHOPPING LIST

Yarn (Medium Weight) MEDIUM 4

[3.5 ounces, 210 yards (100 grams, 192 meters) per skein**]**:

☐ 5 skeins

Crochet Hook

☐ Size I (5.5 mm) **or** size needed for gauge

Additional Supplies

☐ Yarn needle

☐ $^{7}/_{8}$" (22 mm) Buttons - 6

GAUGE INFORMATION

12 dc and 6 rows = 3¼" (8.25 cm)

Gauge Swatch:

2¾" wide x 3¼" high
(7 cm x 8.25 cm)

Work same as Body for 6 rows: 10 dc.

STITCH GUIDE

DOUBLE CROCHET 2 TOGETHER
(abbreviated dc2tog)
(uses 2 dc)

★ YO, insert hook in **next** dc, YO and pull up a loop, YO and draw through 2 loops on hook; repeat from ★ once **more**, YO and draw through all 3 loops on hook **(counts as one dc)**.

The Body begins at a side point. One edge has increases to form the first half of the Shawl, then deceases to form the second half. A Ruffle is worked around the entire edge.

INSTRUCTIONS

BODY

Row 1: Ch 4, 2 dc in fourth ch from hook: 2 dc.

Beginning ch 2 does **not** count as a dc.

Row 2 (Right side)**:** Ch 2, turn; dc in first dc, 3 dc in last dc: 4 dc.

Note: Loop a short piece of yarn around any dc on Row 2 to mark **right** side.

Row 3 (Increase row)**:** Ch 2, turn; 2 dc in first dc, dc in each remaining dc across: 5 dc.

Row 4 (Increase row)**:** Ch 2, turn; dc in each dc across to last dc, 3 dc in last dc: 7 dc.

Rows 5-55: Repeat Rows 3 and 4, 25 times; then repeat Row 3 once **more**: 83 dc.

Note: Place marker in top of first dc made on Row 55 to mark center point and bottom edge of Shawl.

Row 56 (Decrease row)**:** Ch 2, turn; dc in each dc across to last 2 dc, dc2tog: 82 dc.

Row 57 (Decrease row)**:** Ch 2, turn; beginning in first dc, dc2tog twice, dc in each remaining dc across: 80 dc.

Rows 58-108: Repeat Rows 56 and 57, 25 times; then repeat Row 56 once **more**: 4 dc.

Row 109 (Decrease row)**:** Ch 2, turn; beginning in first dc, dc2tog twice: 2 dc.

Row 110: Ch 2, turn; beginning in first dc, dc2tog; do **not** finish off: one dc.

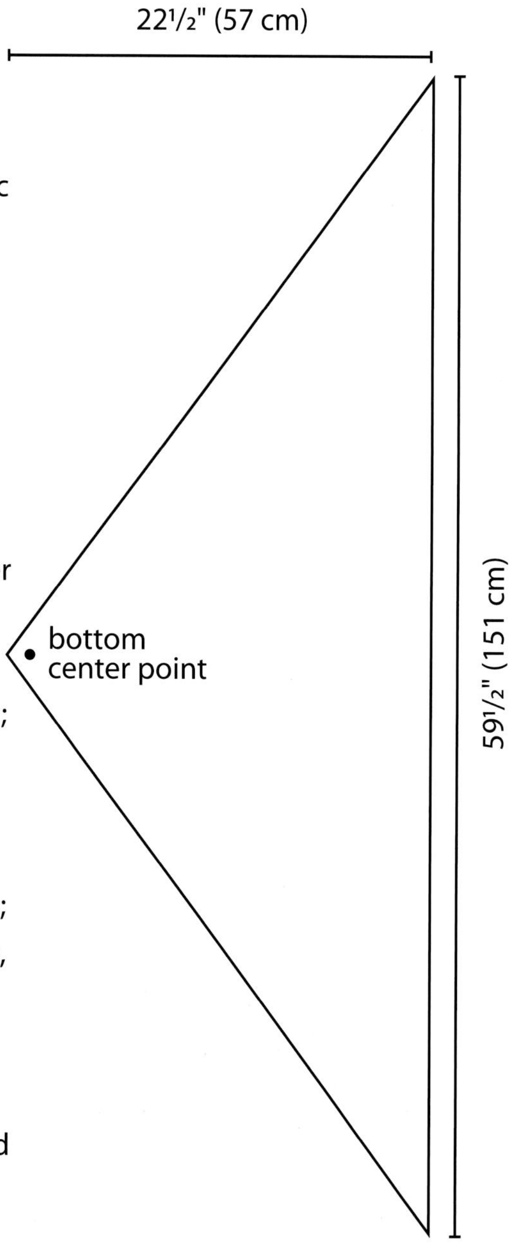

RUFFLE

Rnd 1: Ch 2, do **not** turn; 2 dc in last dc made on Row 110, dc evenly across end of rows to bottom of Row 1 at beginning side point, 5 dc in free loop of ch at beginning point *(Fig. 2, page 30)*, dc evenly across end of rows, 3 dc in same st as first dc; join with slip st to first dc.

Rnd 2: Ch 2, turn; 3 dc in same st as joining and in each of next 2 dc, 2 dc in next dc and in each dc across to next 5-dc group (beginning side point), 2 dc in next dc, 3 dc in each of next 3 dc, 2 dc in next dc and in each dc across to within 1 dc of marked center point on bottom edge, 3 dc in each of next 3 dc, do **not** remove marker, 2 dc in next dc and in each dc across; join with slip st to first dc.

Rnd 3: Ch 2, turn; dc in each dc around; join with slip st to first dc, finish off.

Using Placement Diagram as a guide, sew buttons to **wrong** side of Rnd 1 on the Ruffle, along both sides of center point marker, as follows: sew the first button 2" (5 cm) from the center point marker, then sew on 2 more buttons spacing them 3" (7.5 cm) apart. Repeat on the opposite side of the center point marker.

Use corresponding spaces between dc on Rnd 1 of Ruffle for buttonholes.

PLACEMENT DIAGRAM

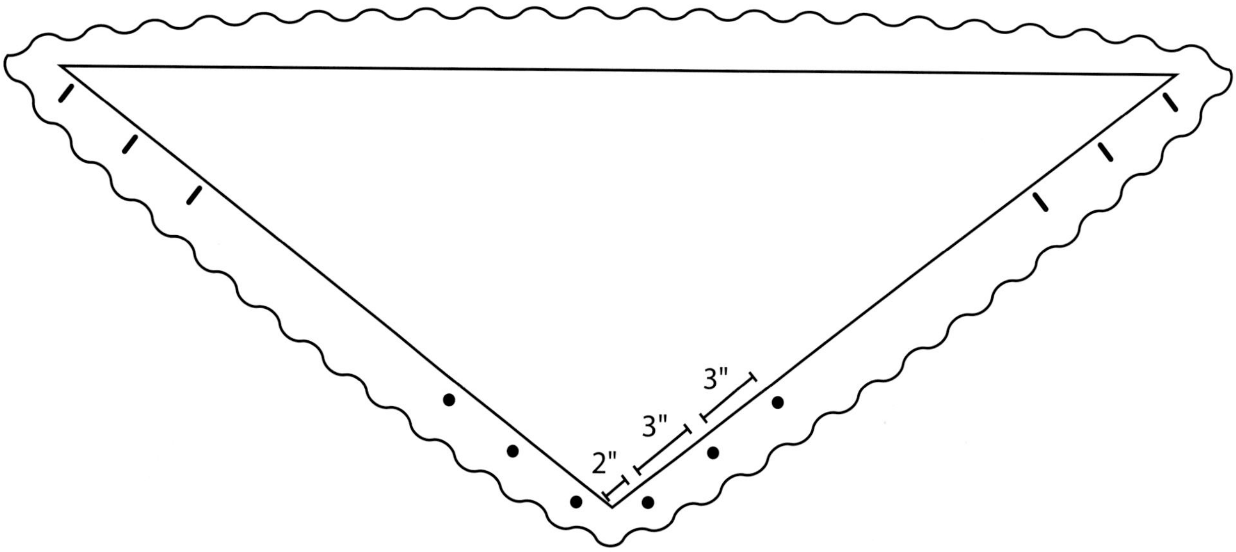

hybrid scarf

EASY

This dramatic scarf is a versatile accessory that can also be worn as a demi shawl. Make it as narrow or as wide as you want, or change the length with easy adjustments; just be sure to buy yarn accordingly.

Finished Size: Approximately 9" wide x 44" long at neck edge (23 cm x 112 cm)

SHOPPING LIST

Yarn (Medium Weight) MEDIUM 4

[3.5 ounces, 151 yards (100 grams, 138 meters) per skein**]**:

- ☐ 3 skeins

Crochet Hook

- ☐ Size K (6.5 mm) **or** size needed for gauge

Additional Supplies

- ☐ Yarn needle
- ☐ $1^1/_8$" (29 mm) Button

GAUGE INFORMATION

10 dc and 6 rows = 4" (10 cm)

Gauge Swatch: 4" (10 cm) square

Ch 12.

Row 1: Dc in third ch from hook and in each ch across: 10 dc.

Beginning ch 2 does **not** count as a dc.

Rows 2-6: Ch 2, turn; dc in each dc across.

Finish off.

INSTRUCTIONS

To adjust the length, add or subtract 22 chains from the beginning chain for approximately every 9" (23 cm) you want to adjust.

Ch 112.

Row 1 (Right side)**:** Dc in third ch from hook and in each ch across: 110 dc.

Note: Loop a short piece of yarn around any dc on Row 1 to mark **right** side.

Beginning ch 2 does **not** count as a dc.

Row 2: Ch 2, turn; dc in each dc across.

Row 3 (Increase row)**:** Ch 2, turn; dc in first 5 dc, 3 dc in next dc, (dc in next 10 dc, 3 dc in next dc) across to last 5 dc, dc in last 5 dc: 130 dc.

Row 4 (Increase row)**:** Ch 2, turn; ★ dc in each dc across to center dc of next 3-dc group, 3 dc in center dc; repeat from ★ 9 times **more**, dc in each remaining dc across: 150 dc.

Repeat Row 4, 8 times **or** until piece measures desired width, ending by working a **wrong** side row.

Edging: Ch 1, turn; sc in first dc, (sc, ch 3, 3 dc) in next dc, ★ skip next 3 dc, (sc, ch 3, 3 dc) in next dc; repeat from ★ across to last 4 dc, skip next 3 dc, sc in last dc; finish off.

With **right** side of piece facing, sew button to Row 2 at top of third dc from either edge. Use corresponding space between dc on opposite end of Row 2 for buttonhole.

button-up poncho

EASY

This unique poncho offers the convenience of a button-up front and the look of roomy sleeves. Optional details include a collar, hood, and stripes.

SHOPPING LIST

Yarn (Medium Weight) MEDIUM 4

SOLID PONCHO

[6 ounces, 315 yards
(170 grams, 288 meters) per skein]:

- ☐ **Plain Neckline** - 4{4-5} skeins
- ☐ **With Collar** - 4{4-5} skeins
- ☐ **With Hood** - 4{5-5} skeins

OR

[3.5 ounces, 218 yards
(100 grams, 200 meters) per skein]:

- ☐ **Plain Neckline** - 7{7-8} skeins
- ☐ **With Collar** - 7{7-8} skeins
- ☐ **With Hood** - 7{8-9} skeins

STRIPED PONCHO

- ☐ Black - 255{275-310} yards/ 233{251-283} meters
- ☐ Scrap colors (as many as desired) - 1,010{1,100-1,230} yards/ 924{1,006-1,125} meters **total**
- ☐ Variegated (as many as desired) - 200{215-240} yards/ 183{197-219} meters **total**

Note: Add 1 ounce/30 grams for a collar or 2{2.5-3} ounces/ 60{70-90} grams for a hood.

Crochet Hook

- ☐ Size I (5.5 mm) **or** size needed for gauge

Additional Supplies

- ☐ Yarn needle
- ☐ 7/8" - 1" (22 mm - 25 mm) Buttons - 5
- ☐ Stitch markers
- ☐ Pins

SIZE INFORMATION

Sizes	Finished Size
Small/Medium	22¼" l x 45" w (56.5 cm x 114.5 cm)
Large/X-Large	22½" l x 49" w (57 cm x 124.5 cm)
2X/3X-Large	23½" l x 53" w (59.5 cm x 134.5 cm)

Size Note: We have printed the instructions for the sizes in different colors to make it easier for you to find:

- Small/Medium in Blue
- Large/X-Large in Pink
- 2X/3X-Large in Green

Instructions in Black apply to all sizes.

GAUGE INFORMATION

13 dc and 8 rows = 4" (10 cm)

Gauge Swatch: 4" (10 cm) square

Ch 15.

Row 1: Dc in third ch from hook and in each ch across: 13 dc.

Beginning ch 2 does **not** count as a dc.

Rows 2-8: Ch 2, turn; dc in each dc across.

Finish off.

STITCH GUIDE

FRONT POST TREBLE CROCHET *(abbreviated FPtr)*

YO twice, insert hook from **front** to **back** around post of st indicated *(Fig. 5, page 31)*, YO and pull up a loop (4 loops on hook), (YO and draw through 2 loops on hook) 3 times.

DOUBLE CROCHET 2 TOGETHER *(abbreviated dc2tog)* (uses 2 dc)

★ YO, insert hook in **next** dc, YO and pull up a loop, YO and draw through 2 loops on hook; repeat from ★ once **more**, YO and draw through all 3 loops on hook **(counts as one dc)**.

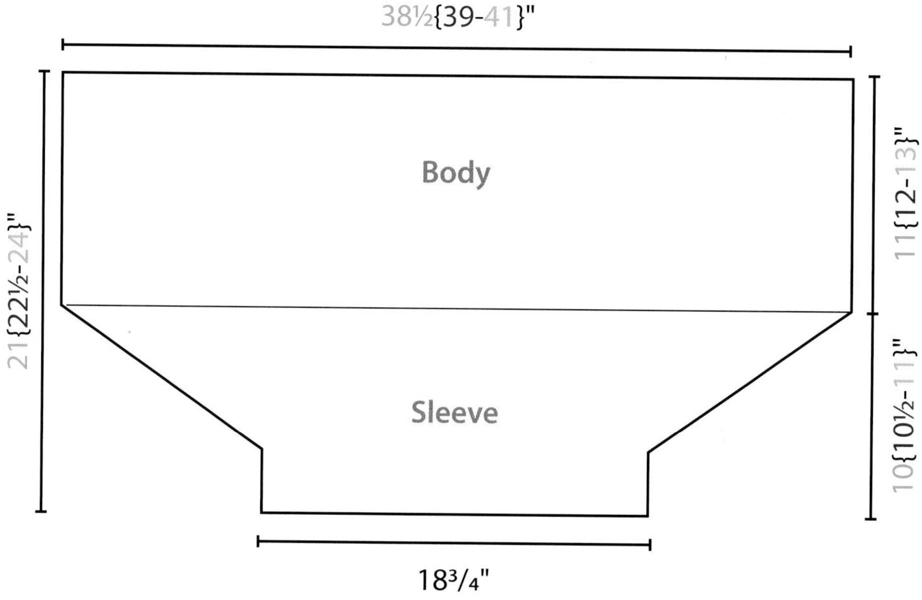

This Poncho is worked in two separate pieces. Each piece begins at the wrist, increasing stitches on each edge to form very wide Sleeves, then working even to form half the Body, ending at the center back of the garment. The two pieces will be sewn together across a portion of the last row, forming the center back seam. Each Sleeve is sewn across the ends of the rows.

The solid poncho, page 23, has mock ribbing at the bottom of the Sleeves and Body and an optional hood or collar.

The striped poncho, page 26, is worked in dc while maintaining a stripe sequence and also has an optional hood or collar.

INSTRUCTIONS for SOLID PONCHO

FIRST HALF

SLEEVE

Ch 63.

Row 1: Dc in third ch from hook and in each ch across: 61 dc.

Beginning ch 2 does **not** count as a dc.

Row 2 (Right side)**:** Ch 2, turn; dc in first dc, ★ work FPtr around next dc, dc in next dc; repeat from ★ across: 31 dc and 30 FPtr.

Row 3: Ch 2, turn; dc in each st across: 61 dc.

Row 4: Ch 2, turn; dc in first dc, ★ work FPtr around FPtr in row **below** next dc, skip dc **behind** FPtr, dc in next dc; repeat from ★ across: 31 dc and 30 FPtr.

Row 5: Ch 2, turn; 2 dc in first dc, dc in each remaining st across to last dc, 2 dc in last dc: 63 dc.

Row 6: Ch 2, turn; 2 dc in first dc, dc in next 12 dc, 2 dc in next dc, (dc in next 11 dc, 2 dc in next dc) 3 times, dc in next 12 dc, 2 dc in last dc: 69 dc.

Row 7: Ch 2, turn; 2 dc in first dc, dc in each remaining dc across to last dc, 2 dc in last dc: 71 dc.

Row 8 (Increase row)**:** Ch 2, turn; 2 dc in first dc, (dc in next 13 dc, 2 dc in next dc) across: 77 dc.

Row 9 (Increase row)**:** Ch 2, turn; 2 dc in first dc, dc in each remaining dc across to last dc, 2 dc in last dc: 79 dc.

Row 10 (Increase row)**:** Work in same manner as Row 8, increasing in first and last dc with 4 more increases evenly spaced between: 85 dc.

Rows 11 thru 20{21-22}: Repeat Rows 9 and 10, 5{5-6} times; then repeat Row 9, 0{1-0} time(s) **more** *(see Zeros, page 29)*: 125{127-133} dc.

Note: Place a marker in first and last dc on last row to mark end of Sleeve.

BODY

Row 1: Ch 2, turn; dc in each dc across.

Repeat Row 1, 21{23-25} times **or** until Body measures desired width.

Finish off.

SECOND HALF

Work same as First Half.

ASSEMBLY

Place the Body of both pieces with **wrong** sides together. Using the placement diagram as a guide, pin pieces together across the last row to about 3½" (9 cm) before center. Working through **both** loops of **both** pieces, whipstitch Body pieces together *(Fig. 6a, page 31)*, keeping the sewing yarn fairly loose.

With **wrong** sides together and beginning at the Sleeve edge, whipstitch seam to the marked stitch *(Fig. 6b, page 31)*.

PLACEMENT DIAGRAM

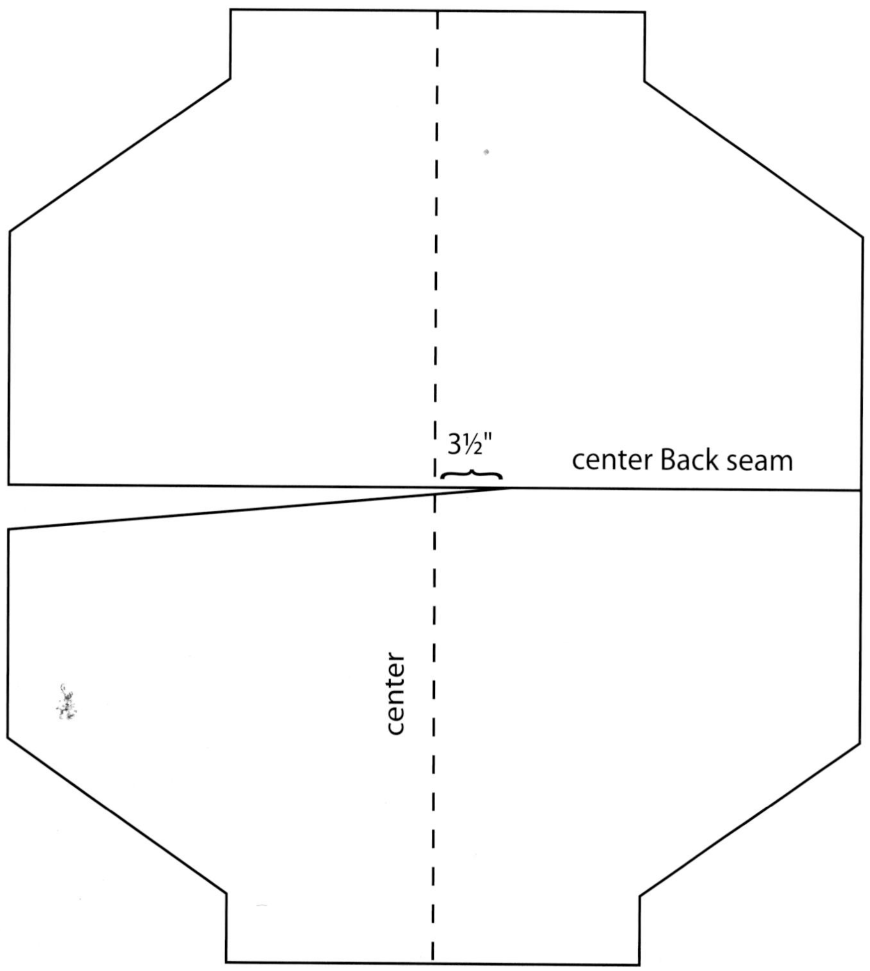

BOTTOM BAND

Row 1: With **wrong** side facing and working in end of rows on Body, join yarn with dc in first row *(Fig. 4, page 31)*; dc evenly across bottom edge making sure to have an odd number of stitches.

Row 2: Ch 2, turn; dc in first dc, ★ work FPtr around next dc, dc in next dc; repeat from ★ across.

Row 3: Ch 2, turn; dc in each st across.

Row 4: Ch 2, turn; dc in first dc, ★ work FPtr around FPtr in row **below** next dc, skip dc **behind** FPtr, dc in next dc; repeat from ★ across.

Rows 5 and 6: Repeat Rows 3 and 4; do **not** finish off.

FRONT BAND

Row 1: Ch 1, do **not** turn; sc evenly spaced across end of rows on Bottom Band, sc in each dc across Body to Bottom Band on opposite side, sc evenly spaced across end of rows.

Row 2: Ch 1, turn; sc in each sc across.

Row 3: Ch 1, turn; sc in first 3 sc, ch 2, skip next 2 sc (for buttonhole), ★ sc in next 9 sc, ch 2, skip next 2 sc; repeat from ★ 3 times **more**, sc in each remaining sc across: 5 buttonholes made.

Row 4: Ch 1, turn; sc in each sc across working 2 sc in each ch-2 sp.

Row 5: Ch 1, turn; sc in each sc across; finish off.

Sew 5 buttons on left Front Band matching buttonholes.

COLLAR

Row 1: With **right** side facing, count 20{25-30} sc on Front Band from right hand side of center Back and join yarn with dc in same st; dc in next 39{49-59} sc: 40{50-60} dc.

Rows 2 thru 5{6-7}: Ch 2, turn; 2 dc in first dc, dc in each remaining dc across to last dc, 2 dc in last dc: 48{60-72} dc.

Finish off.

HOOD

Row 1: With **right** side facing, count 20{25-30} sc on Front Band from right hand side of center Back and join yarn with dc in same st; dc in next 39{49-59} sc: 40{50-60} dc.

Rows 2-22: Ch 2, turn; dc in each dc across.

Row 23: Ch 2, turn; dc in first 18{23-28} dc, dc2tog twice, dc in each remaining dc across: 38{48-58} dc.

Row 24: Ch 2, turn; dc in first 17{22-27} dc, dc2tog twice, dc in each remaining dc across; finish off leaving long end for sewing: 36{46-56} dc.

Fold Hood in half with **wrong** side together and matching dc on last row; whipstitch top seam.

TRIM

With **right** side of Hood facing, join yarn with dc in base of first dc on Row 1 of Hood; working in end of rows, dc evenly across Hood ending at base of last dc on Row 1; finish off.

INSTRUCTIONS for STRIPED PONCHO

FIRST HALF

CHANGING COLORS

YO, insert hook in next dc, YO and pull up a loop (3 loops on hook), YO and draw through 2 loops on hook, cut yarn; with new yarn, YO and draw through both loops on hook *(Fig. A)*.

Fig. A

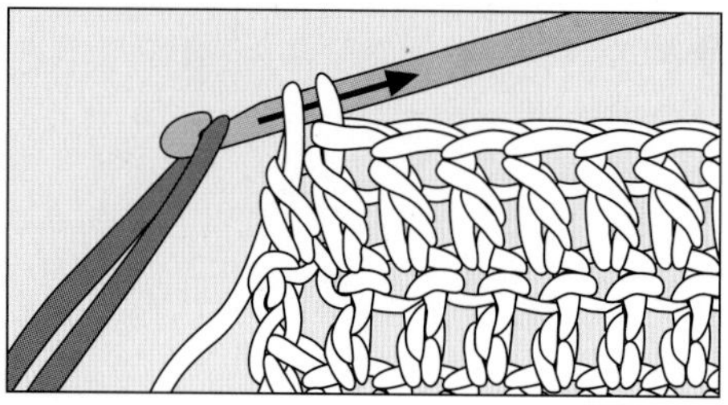

STRIPE SEQUENCE

★ 2 Rows Scrap Color, 1 row Variegated, 2 rows Scrap Color, 1 row Black; repeat from ★ throughout.

SLEEVE

Working in stripe sequence, ch 63.

Row 1: Dc in third ch from hook and in each ch across: 61 dc.

Beginning ch 2 does **not** count as a dc.

Row 2 (Right side)**:** Ch 2, turn; dc in each dc across changing colors in last dc.

Note: Loop a short piece of yarn around any dc on Row 2 to mark **right** side.

Row 3: Ch 2, turn; dc in each dc across changing colors in last dc.

Continue to change colors in same manner throughout.

Row 4: Ch 2, turn; dc in each dc across.

Row 5: Ch 2, turn; 2 dc in first dc, dc in each remaining dc across to last dc, 2 dc in last dc: 63 dc.

Row 6: Ch 2, turn; 2 dc in first dc, dc in next 12 dc, 2 dc in next dc, (dc in next 11 dc, 2 dc in next dc) 3 times, dc in next 12 dc, 2 dc in last dc: 69 dc.

Row 7: Ch 2, turn; 2 dc in first dc, dc in each remaining dc across to last dc, 2 dc in last dc: 71 dc.

Row 8 (Increase row)**:** Ch 2, turn; 2 dc in first dc, (dc in next 13 dc, 2 dc in next dc) across: 77 dc.

Row 9 (Increase row)**:** Ch 2, turn; 2 dc in first dc, dc in each remaining dc across to last dc, 2 dc in last dc: 79 dc.

Row 10 (Increase row)**:** Work in same manner as Row 8, increasing in first and last dc with 4 more increases evenly spaced between: 85 dc.

Rows 11 thru 20{21-22}: Repeat Rows 9 and 10, 5{5-6} times; then Repeat Row 9, 0{1-0} time(s) **more** *(see Zeros, page 29)*: 125{127-133} dc.

Note: Place a marker in first and last dc on last row to mark end of Sleeve.

BODY

Continue working in established stripe sequence.

Row 1: Ch 2, turn; dc in each dc across.

Repeat Row 1, 21{23-25} times **or** until Body measures desired width.

Finish off.

SECOND HALF

Work same as First Half.

ASSEMBLY

Place the Body of both pieces with **wrong** sides together. Using the placement diagram as a guide, page 24, pin pieces together across the last row to about 3½" (9 cm) before center. Working through **both** loops of **both** pieces, whipstitch Body pieces together *(Fig. 6a, page 31)*, keeping the sewing yarn fairly loose.

With **wrong** sides together and beginning at the Sleeve edge, whipstitch seam to the marked stitch *(Fig. 6b, page 31)*.

BOTTOM BAND

Row 1: With **right** side facing and working in end of rows on Body, join Black with dc in first row *(Fig. 4, page 31)*; dc evenly across bottom edge.

Row 2: Ch 2, turn; dc in each dc across.

Repeat Row 2, 1 or 3 times, as desired, ending by working a **right** side row; do **not** finish off.

FRONT BAND

Row 1: Ch 1, do **not** turn; sc evenly spaced across end of rows on Bottom Band, sc in each dc across Body to Bottom Band on opposite side, sc evenly spaced across end of rows.

Row 2: Ch 1, turn; sc in each sc across.

Row 3: Ch 1, turn; sc in first 3 sc, ch 2, skip next 2 sc (for buttonhole), ★ sc in next 9 sc, ch 2, skip next 2 sc; repeat from ★ 3 times **more**, sc in each remaining sc across: 5 buttonholes made.

Row 4: Ch 1, turn; sc in each sc across working 2 sc in each ch-2 sp.

Row 5: Ch 1, turn; sc in each sc across; finish off.

Sew 5 buttons on left Front Band matching buttonholes.

COLLAR OR HOOD

Work same as Solid Poncho, page 25, if desired.

general instructions

ABBREVIATIONS

ch	chain(s)
cm	centimeters
dc	double crochet(s)
dc2tog	double crochet 2 together
FPtr	Front Post treble crochet(s)
mm	millimeters
Rnd(s)	Round(s)
sc	single crochet(s)
sp(s)	space(s)
st(s)	stitch(es)
YO	yarn over

SYMBOLS & TERMS

★ — work instructions following ★ as many **more** times as indicated in addition to the first time.

( ) or **[ ]** — work enclosed instructions **as many** times as specified by the number immediately following **or** work all enclosed instructions in stitch or space indicated **or** contains explanatory remarks.

colon (:) — the number(s) given after a colon at the end of a row or round denote(s) the number of stitches you should have on that row or round.

GAUGE

Exact gauge is **essential** for proper size. Before beginning your project, make the sample swatch given in the individual instructions in the yarn and hook specified. After completing the swatch, measure it, counting your stitches and rows carefully. If your swatch is larger or smaller than specified, **make another, changing hook size to get the correct gauge**. Keep trying until you find the size hook that will give you the specified gauge.

ZEROS

To consolidate the length of an involved pattern, zeros are sometimes used so that all sizes can be combined. For example, repeat Row 9, 0{1-0} time(s) **more** means that the first and third sizes would do nothing, and the second size would repeat Row 9 once.

CROCHET TERMINOLOGY		
UNITED STATES		INTERNATIONAL
slip stitch (slip st)	=	single crochet (sc)
single crochet (sc)	=	double crochet (dc)
half double crochet (hdc)	=	half treble crochet (htr)
double crochet (dc)	=	treble crochet(tr)
treble crochet (tr)	=	double treble crochet (dtr)
double treble crochet (dtr)	=	triple treble crochet (ttr)
triple treble crochet (tr tr)	=	quadruple treble crochet (qtr)
skip	=	miss

BACK LOOP ONLY

Work only in loop(s) indicated by arrow *(Fig. 1)*.

Fig. 1

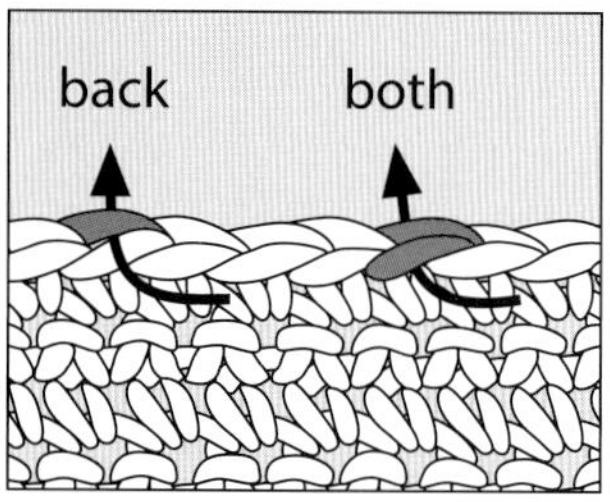

FREE LOOPS OF A CHAIN

When instructed to work in free loops of a chain, work in loop indicated by arrow *(Fig. 2)*.

Fig. 2

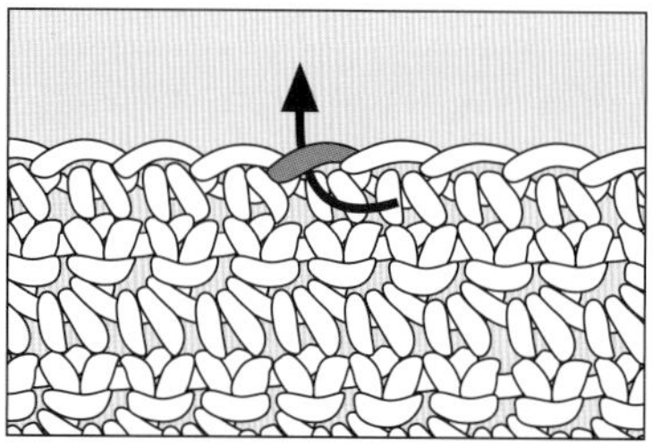

JOINING WITH SC

When instructed to join with sc, begin with a slip knot on hook. Insert hook in stitch or space indicated, YO and pull up a loop, YO and draw through both loops on hook *(Figs. 3a & b)*.

Fig. 3a

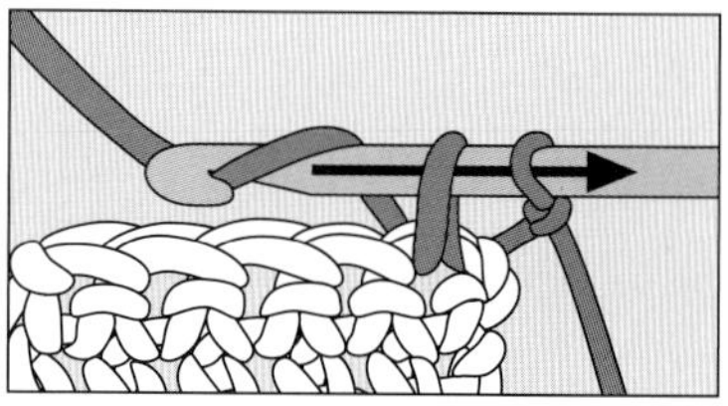

Fig. 3b

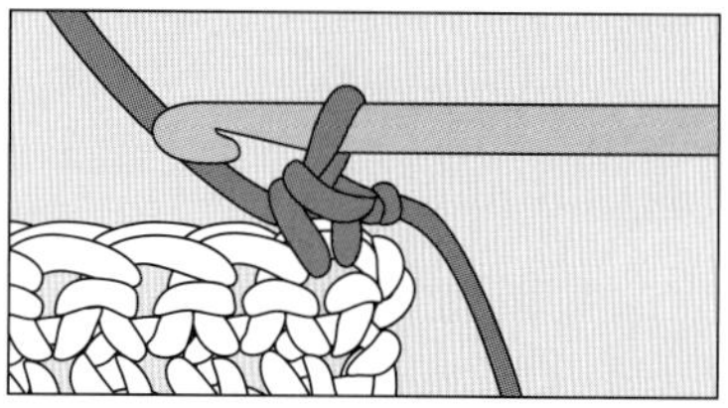

Yarn Weight Symbol & Names	LACE 0	SUPER FINE 1	FINE 2	LIGHT 3	MEDIUM 4	BULKY 5	SUPER BULKY 6
Type of Yarns in Category	Fingering, 10-count crochet thread	Sock, Fingering Baby	Sport, Baby	DK, Light Worsted	Worsted, Afghan, Aran	Chunky, Craft, Rug	Bulky, Roving
Crochet Gauge* Ranges in Single Crochet to 4" (10 cm)	32-42 double crochets**	21-32 sts	16-20 sts	12-17 sts	11-14 sts	8-11 sts	5-9 sts
Advised Hook Size Range	Steel*** 6,7,8 Regular hook B-1	B-1 to E-4	E-4 to 7	7 to I-9	I-9 to K-10.5	K-10.5 to M-13	M-13 and larger

*GUIDELINES ONLY: The chart above reflects the most commonly used gauges and hook sizes for specific yarn categories.

** Lace weight yarns are usually crocheted on larger-size hooks to create lacy openwork patterns. Accordingly, a gauge range is difficult to determine. Always follow the gauge stated in your pattern.

*** Steel crochet hooks are sized differently from regular hooks–the higher the number the smaller the hook, which is the reverse of regular hook sizing.

CROCHET HOOKS

U.S.	B-1	C-2	D-3	E-4	F-5	G-6	H-8	I-9	J-10	K-10½	L-11	M/N-13	N/P-15	P/Q	Q	S
Metric - mm	2.25	2.75	3.25	3.5	3.75	4	5	5.5	6	6.5	8	9	10	15	16	19

BEGINNER	Projects for first-time crocheters using basic stitches. Minimal shaping.
EASY	Projects using yarn with basic stitches, repetitive stitch patterns, simple color changes, and simple shaping and finishing.
INTERMEDIATE	Projects using a variety of techniques, such as basic lace patterns or color patterns, mid-level shaping and finishing.
EXPERIENCED	Projects with intricate stitch patterns, techniques and dimension, such as non-repeating patterns, multi-color techniques, fine threads, small hooks, detailed shaping and refined finishing.

JOINING WITH DC

When instructed to join with dc, begin with a slip knot on hook. YO, holding loop on hook, insert hook in stitch or space indicated, YO and pull up a loop (3 loops on hook), (YO and draw through 2 loops on hook) twice *(Fig. 4)*.

Fig. 4

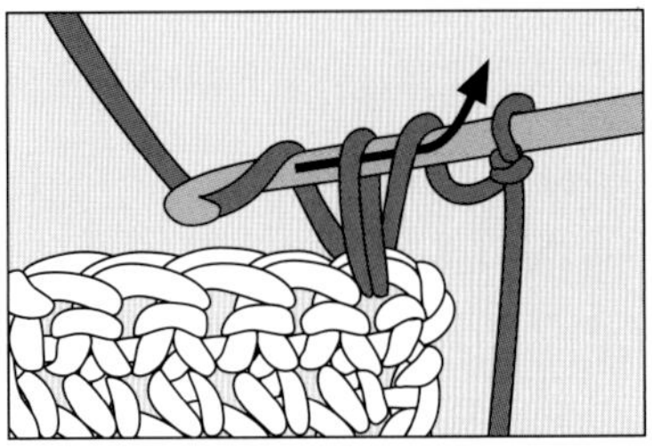

FRONT POST STITCH

Work around post of stitch indicated, inserting hook in direction of arrow *(Fig. 5)*.

Fig. 5

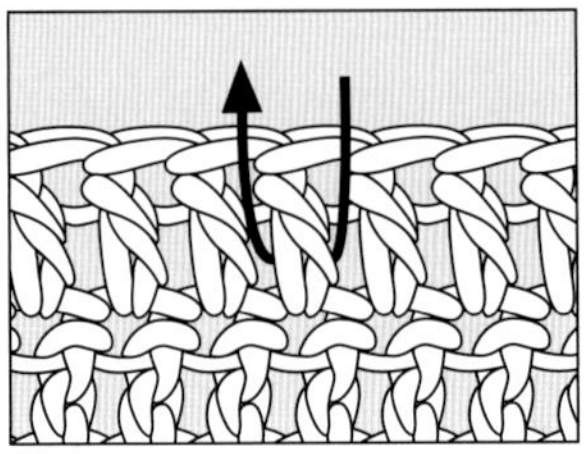

WHIPSTITCH

With **wrong** sides together, sew through both pieces once to secure the beginning of the seam, leaving an ample yarn end to weave in later. Insert the needle from **back** to **front** through **both** loops of each stitch on **both** pieces *(Fig. 6a)*, or in end of rows *(Fig. 6a)*. Bring the needle around and insert it from **back** to **front** through the next strands on both pieces. Continue in same manner, keeping the sewing yarn fairly loose.

Fig. 6a

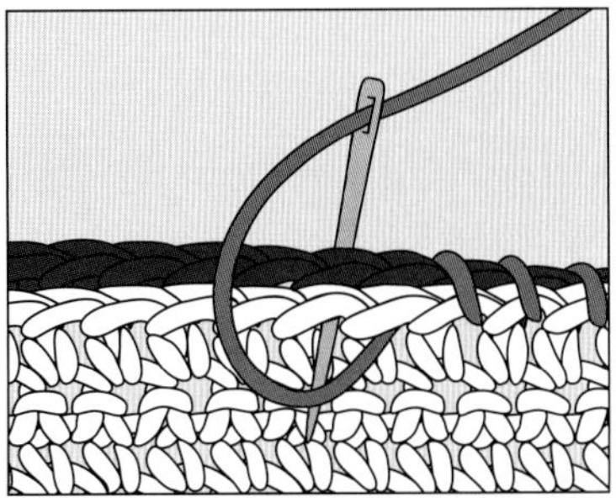

Fig. 6b

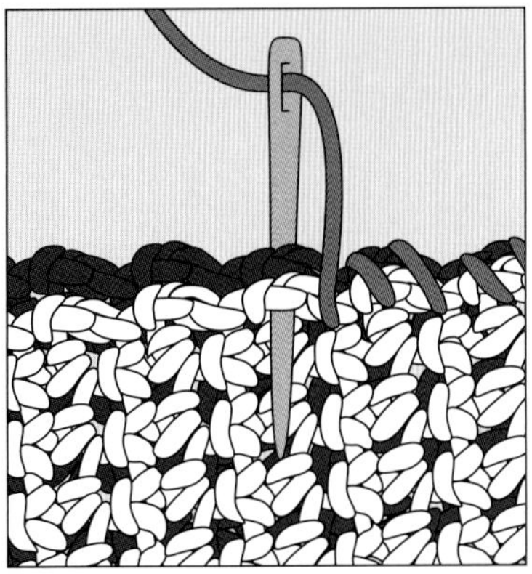

MEET THE DESIGNER

When Shelle Hendrix sees a need, she often turns to crochet to find a solution. That's how the Cuffed Shawl came to be designed.

"I dislike wearing coats in the winter, so I came up with a loose-fitting shawl which is warm yet not confining," Shelle said. "The cuffed sleeves help keep it in place as you move about."

Her interest in crochet began in 1972, when she wanted to make a blanket for her first child and asked her mother-in-law to teach her. These days, she enjoys crocheting an eclectic mix of casual, fun items for family, pets, and dolls. Her other Leisure Arts books include *Dashing Doggie Duds, Crochet Wraps for Dolly and Me, Completely Cozy Wraps to Crochet, Oodles of Outerwear for Canines to Knit*, and two volumes of *Hats and Diaper Covers*.

Four grandchildren and a houseful of pets keep Shelle hopping, but the Indiana resident also teaches guitar and piano and works part-time as an activities leader and driver at a nursing home. Look for Shelle on Facebook and Ravelry (user name shelleden), or visit queeniescabin.blogspot.com and shelleden.etsy.com.

yarn information

The items in this book were made using medium and bulky weight yarn. Any brand of medium or bulky weight yarn may be used. It is best to refer to the yardage/meters when determining how many skeins or balls to purchase. Remember, to arrive at the finished size, it is the GAUGE/TENSION that is important, not the brand of yarn.

For your convenience, listed below are the yarns used to create our photography models.

CUFFED SHAWL

With Plain Neckline:
Lion Brand® Tweed Stripes®
#206 Woodlands
With Hood:
Lion Brand® Homespun®
#302 Colonial **or**
#413 Marble

RUFFLED SHAWL

Patons® Classic Wool Worsted
#00229 Natural Mix

HYBRID SCARF

Red Heart® Boutique™ Treasure™
#1930 Horizon

BUTTON-UP PONCHO

Solid with Collar:
Caron® Simply Soft®
#9710 Country Blue
Solid with Hood:
Red Heart® Collage™
#2352 Crimson Maple
Striped with Plain Neckline:
Lion Brand® Vanna's Choice®
and *Red Heart® Super Saver®*
Black, and assorted
Variegated and Scrap colors

We have made every effort to ensure that these instructions are accurate and complete. We cannot, however, be responsible for human error, typographical mistakes, or variations in individual work.

Production Team: Writer/Technical Editor - Cathy Hardy; Editorial Writer - Susan Frantz Wiles; Senior Graphic Artist - Lora Puls; Graphic Artist - Stacy Owens; Photo Stylist - Lori Wenger; and Photographer - Jason Masters.